War D...

by Robert Marshall Allan • Anna Eisenmenger •
Harry Frieman

TABLE OF CONTENTS

Introduction

FROM 1914 to 1918, most of the world was engaged in a deadly war. It started in Europe, between one group of countries that called themselves the Allied powers and another group of countries that called themselves the Central powers. The main countries in the Allied powers were France, Great Britain, Russia, and the United States. The main Central powers consisted of Germany, **Austria-Hungary**, Bulgaria, and the **Ottoman Empire**. The war eventually spread to Africa and Asia. This was the First World War.

In the years leading up to the war, European nations attempted to expand, and to build their power. They used three methods to increase their power: building up their armies, adding new colonies, and **annexing** land from existing countries. To protect their own lands from encroachment, neighboring countries sought alliances with other countries. With nations vying for power and creating alliances, Europe was quickly divided into sides. Alliances made heads of state overconfident because they had support. Countries heightened their military preparation. Leaders from all sides were convinced of their superiority, and that any war would be short-lived.

The Great War Alliances

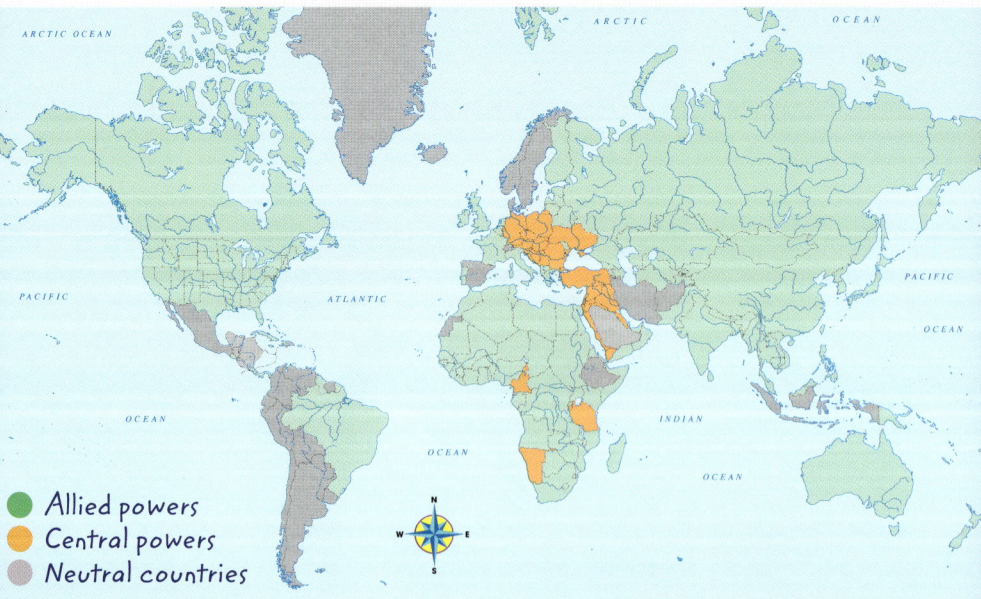

- 🟢 Allied powers
- 🟠 Central powers
- ⚪ Neutral countries

Austria-Hungary a large empire that had land from present-day Italy to eastern Europe and the Baltics, often shortened to "Austria"
Ottoman Empire present-day Turkey

War began when the heir to the throne of Austria-Hungary, Archduke Franz Ferdinand, was assassinated by a Serbian terrorist. Austria, wanting to show its might, declared war on Serbia. Russia was allied to Serbia, so it declared war on Austria. Germany was aligned with Austria, and so it declared war on Russia as well as Russia's other ally, France. To get to France quickly, Germany had to invade Belgium, which was a neutral country. Great Britain had previously made a deal to protect Belgium, so it entered the war. Italy wanted some land

from Austria and joined the Allies in 1915. The United States joined the Allies two years later when a German submarine sank a ship carrying American citizens.

At the time that it was happening, World War I was called "the Great War." One hundred and thirty-five countries from across the globe became involved in the conflict, and 16 million people lost their lives—only 9.7 million of them soldiers. Though there were battles all over the world, the majority of fighting took place in the stretch of land from France to Russia.

The introduction of new weaponry increased the number of lives lost. Long-range guns meant one didn't have to get as close to an enemy to fire, and railroads made it easier to transport troops and heavy machinery. Armored tanks, submarines, and airplanes became standard during the war, as did the use of poison gas. To protect their fighters from attacks at long distances, armies built **trenches** from which soldiers could shoot and be protected.

In the end, the Central powers surrendered. Germany signed an **armistice** with the Allied powers that ended the fighting at 11 a.m. on November 11, 1918.

The chapters that follow contain the real diaries and letters of three people involved in World War I: Robert Marshall Allan, Anna Eisenmenger, and Harry Frieman. These excerpts have retained the original spellings and phrasings of the time.

Robert Marshall Allan

ROBERT Marshall Allan (1886–1946) was a physician and medical professor from South Brisbane, Australia. He studied medicine at the University of Edinburgh in Scotland, and then worked as a **resident** in Dublin, Ireland. Allan toured Europe teaching medicine before he enlisted as a lieutenant in the Royal Army Medical Corps in 1914.

During World War I, Allan served in France for fourteen months. He was sent to **Mesopotamia**, and eventually to India. He wrote letters to his father during this time, which were published anonymously by Watson Ferguson & Co. in two volumes: *Letters From a Young Queenslander* (1915) and *Mesopotamia and India* (1916).

After the armistice, he returned to Brisbane, where he practiced as a medical specialist. On November 9, 1920, Allan married Maryanne Eleanor Dines Bracker. They had two children. Throughout his life, Allan continued to move up through the military, hospital, and collegiate ranks, earning various honors and positions.

Indian Ocean

OCEAN

AUSTRALIA

Brisbane

resident a medical graduate serving in a hospital while completing a residency; this must be done before one becomes a doctor

Mesopotamia the old name for an area of southeast Asia that is now present-day Iraq

September 11, 1914

This is a training centre for infantry and **artillery**. We form part of the next Division to go abroad—the **First Division of Kitchener's Army**. They should be ready early in January but long before that I hope to be shifted on nearer the front. I have charge of 2,500 men, and the married quarters in addition. Everything is in a chaotic condition, and it could not well be otherwise. They get as many recruits in a day as in a year previously, and with most of the regulars away, it makes things harder for those left behind. As **red tape** is not altogether absent, delays are still common.

On the whole the men are a very fine lot, keen as mustard and learning quickly. But there are some awful crocks. How they were medically passed beats me, and my present job is to weed them out. The **War Office** objected up till this week to wholesale discharging of men, but now they have got so many good men coming forward, they have allowed us a freer hand, and we can discharge any one. This **Battalion** is a mixture of good men and rotters. . . . So far, I have got rid of 40.

Most of the men arrive with only what they are standing in. The weather has been cold and wet recently, and as they are out all day drilling, there has been a plentiful crop of colds and bronchitis. Friends are sending shirts, socks, etc., and soon each man should have a change. This is no joke for them. Many hours are spent in drill, but the majority are keen, and there are few slackers.

First Division of Kitchener's Army Kitchener's Army was an all-volunteer army named after the British secretary of state for war, Horatio Kitchener; a division is a large military unit consisting of 10,000–30,000 troops.

red tape a phrase usually applied to government that implies rigid control and excessive regulation; it tends to prevent anything (such as legislation) from moving forward

War Office a department of the British Government responsible for the British army

battalion a military unit consisting of 300–1,200 soldiers; several battalions form a regiment

Aldershot, September 23, 1914

Our officers are a fine lot—young fellows—many of them home on leave from India. We have great times of an evening, **yarning** and poking fun at each other. They help one in every way they can, and I often get hints about army etiquette, about which I am naturally ignorant. There are 110,000 recruits here, and the place resounds with drill instructors.

October 1, 1914

Last Saturday the King reviewed the battalions. It was a brilliant day, and the boys did look well. They have been training very hard, and all were keen to see the King. He was accompanied by the Queen, Princess Mary, and Kitchener. They walked along the front line, and then got in motors and drove off. The boys were very disappointed, for most of them only saw the Queen's parasol. While the King certainly had a lot to do, we had hoped that he would have ridden down all the ranks. The men wanted to see their King—and all the majority got was two hours on the parade ground.

October 8, 1914

Yesterday an **RAMC** major inspected what we had done. He also asked if we wanted to stay with the **regiment** or go on soon to the front. I chose the **latter**. It would be pleasant to stay here with the men, and go on in the spring under good weather conditions. But I feel I should go, and I want to. My French and German should be of great use to me. This may be the last long letter from me for some time.

yarning telling long, unbelievable stories
RAMC the Royal Army Medical Corps; a special medical unit of the British Army

Southampton, October 9, 1914

Just a few lines before we go aboard. I had only two hours' notice yesterday. The officers in my mess were kind enough to say how sorry they were to lose me. . . .

Then down to the station—no bands—no cheering crowds—just on to the train and off. I am not going light hearted, nor am I funked. But this Continental trip is something different from any of my others. It will be no picnic—I shall probably have a tremendous amount to do—but I feel that I shall be able to do it. As a grim reminder I have my **identification disc** round my neck. . . .

Our little party promises good—two of the men are Irish, the others a Canadian, an Englishman, and an Australian. So we represent the **Empire** pretty well.

November 9, 1914

Yesterday we got an RAMC man from the front. They have a pretty rough time of it, little better than the troops as regards to danger. The Germans **shell** every main road, dropping shells at intervals all along it. No wounded can be shifted from the trenches in the day time. At night the doctors go up, and often are fired on.

Now for a description of our daily life. I believe that folks at home have heard all sorts of tales about the poor treatment, and even worse of our sick. As far as I have seen, that is all **bunkum**. The British RAMC is really marvellously organised. The war is an abnormal one, so there will be mistakes made.

identification disc also known as a dog tag; a metal disc worn around the neck by soldiers to help identify the bodies of the dead and wounded; they also contain medical information

Empire The British Empire included the United Kingdom, Canada, Australia, New Zealand, India, and South Africa, among others.

shell to drop a bomb or other kind of artillery

bunkum nonsense

When a man is wounded in the trenches he lies there all day. His regimental doctor gives him first aid if he is there, otherwise at night. Parties then come up from the clearing hospital and remove the cases. These hospitals renew dressings, and classify all the men. Only very urgent cases are operated on by them. Then the wounded leave by motor to the nearest station, or are put straight on the hospital trains. These are staffed by doctors and nurses, and run to **Boulogne**. Here the wounded are distributed to the various hospitals. Considering the fierce fighting and the constant shelling of main roads it is a wonder the wounded ever get here. I must say the men at the front do their work exceedingly well.

Boulogne a city in northern France

January 1, 1915

In my line of trenches the water was three feet deep. You can imagine what it must be like in this climate. The men came out in slime up to their necks. Most men smear Vaseline over themselves before dressing, but the water gets through. Conditions have changed considerably since the first months. Then we had no reserves, and the men had to stay weeks in the trenches, without relief—now there is a very good scheme of short spells at work, and then rest.

January 20, 1915

Since last writing I have been right into it. My letters from now on will have to be more discreet than ever, but I have my diary, and that holds everything. . . .

We passed through villages which had been shelled. All along the road we saw the reserve trenches half full of water. There were also graves of soldiers of various nationalities, each with a plain cross, and often a cap hanging on it. . . .

My first post was in a fine house rather than an exposed position. We had funk holes, or dugouts behind for emergency use. At night we had to block up all windows in order to prevent our lights from being seen. My job was to go out at night to the regimental aid post and remove the wounded. An aid post is where the regimental doctor is, and to where his stretcher bearers bring the wounded from the trenches. It is supposed to be out of range of fire, if possible—mine wasn't.

February 12, 1915

What a curious life it is here, and how one gets used to it, and just walks about heedless of the shells. It is difficult to give you a picture of the actual front. Just a stretch of flat country, intersected by trees and ruined houses. About half a mile away is a ruin and some battered houses—there are the reserves, and in front of them the trenches. One hundred and fifty yards in front of them are the Germans. Between is a sea of mud. Nothing more **dismal** and depressing could be imagined than this black country of France. We must stay

in cold rooms all day, as we cannot have smoke issuing out of the chimneys. At night we warm up. . . .

At night everything is black. One hears the challenge of sentries and the answers. Flares go up from the trenches and light up the country with a ghostly bluish-white light, throwing into relief the dark outline of farm houses. Crack, crack go the rifles, and the rapid staccato stutter of the maxims occasionally is heard. Parties of men walk past in the gloom, going down or returning from digging trenches, or relieving those in them, and sometimes stretcher bearers bring up wounded to me. True it is a weird and unnatural existence, but somehow one seems to have always been at it. This slow waiting game has no glories, but sometime soon we shall begin, and the medical staff will be overworked. We all believe the end will come sooner than we expect, and we live in that hope.

May 15, 1915

The plain truth of the fighting recently is, that instead of pushing the Germans, we are being put to our utmost to hold them in. Don't think I am being **despondent**, but when one has been battered about as I was recently it certainly destroys optimistic feelings. As I write the big guns are thundering out again, preparatory to another attack. The country is looking very well just now. The trees have become covered with leaves under a blue sky. **Flanders** looks pretty, and what a contrast to the winter. But within three miles thousands of corpses lie unburied, and more are added to them daily.

August 16, 1915

Sitting back here on a fine afternoon it is hard to realise a war is on. Nobody pays much attention to the aeroplanes overhead. Even big shells landing in the fields do not disturb the harvesters unless they come very close. . . .

The houses are mere shells, the roofs are skeletons of rafters, walls mostly non-existent. In many cases all that remains of the house is a heap of bricks. Trenches run in all directions, and sandbag barricades block the roads. Nothing is visible during the day save clouds of dust as shells burst. At night the roads are dotted with parties coming and going. Starlight shells light everything up, and bullets whizz over, humming like **bluebottles**. Shell holes abound, and little graves and discarded provisions. When the war is over, it will take time to obliterate this awful zone which exists from the sea to Switzerland.

Flanders a region of northern Belgium
bluebottles a type of fly with a metallic blue abdomen

Anna Eisenmenger

ANNA Eisenmenger was a housewife who lived in Vienna, Austria, during World War I. She documented her life and struggles in diaries dating from 1914 to 1924. These diaries were compiled into a collection titled *Blockade: The Diary of an Austrian Middle-Class Woman 1914–1924*. The first American edition was published in 1932.

Eisenmenger wrote her own introduction to the collection, dedicating her diaries to all of the women in the world. Eisenmenger had four children: Liesbeth, Karl, Otto, and Erni, and one son-in-law, Rudi. Her husband was a physician who died in 1918.

During much of the war, Eisenmenger was left on her own to support her children and her grandchild, Wolfgang. Following her husband's death, family responsibilities fell to her, as many of her children returned from the war injured. Her three sons and one son-in-law fought in the war. Liesbeth gave birth to a daughter, but died soon after. Karl suffered from extreme **post-traumatic stress disorder**. Rudi, her son-in-law, lost a leg. Erni returned from the war blind in both eyes. Otto was missing on the Russian front for several years, and it was assumed he died. It is unclear what happened to Eisenmenger and her family after 1924.

post-traumatic stress disorder a mental condition that occurs after a highly stressful and emotional event such as a war; this condition can cause extreme depression, anxiety, flashbacks, and nightmares

Preface

Before me lies a collection of little black diaries. . . . Every word is burnt into my soul. They tell of events and experiences during the World War and the post-war years, experiences which at that time gave an aim and a purpose to my life, the life of an Austrian middle-class woman. They tell of my struggle against the want and misery of the war and post-war years. During the first years this struggle was waged mainly against the want and misery of others. Later it became a desperate struggle against the poverty and distress which daily threatened to deprive me and those dear to me not only of all our material resources but of life itself. . . .

On July 28th, a big industrialist who was staying in our hotel received news that war had been declared against Serbia. At once the heated debates for and against war were silenced. Everyone thought only for himself and how to safeguard his interests. Everyone hastily reflected what was the best course to take, and almost all came to the same conclusion—to leave immediately. The hotel-keeper wrung his hands; his season was ruined. Luggage was hurriedly packed; the telephone and telegraph offices were **besieged**, and every available vehicle was hired, for regular train service was suspended owing to the transport of troops. . . .

Then followed the declarations of war, one after the other, until we found ourselves allied with Germany, Bulgaria and Turkey in a war against the whole world. The five men of my family—my husband, my son-in-law, and my three sons—were in the direct service of the war-fury.

October 25, 1918
Alarming news from the front.
Food situation increasingly difficult.

At last a letter from Karl, delivered to us by one of his comrades on the journey to the Western Front. . . . Karl's letter breathes the deepest depression. He is stationed near **Sette Communi**. They are standing up to their knees in water. He asks for shoes, as his own have rotted through being **incessantly** damp. "The life here is unworthy of any human being. I ask myself again and again how the **motley** collection of older men and young boys in these front positions endure this life. Insufficient food, tattered shoes and uniforms. No possibility of keeping one's self clean. Are our human sensibilities already utterly stupefied?" Poor Karl. If I had any say in the matter, I should be in favour of concluding peace immediately. **Wilson, with his Fourteen Points**, offered us a good, honourable peace. Why didn't we grasp at it? In a postscript Karl writes: "I feel convinced that we can't go on like this. The War will end soon, one way or another. See that you get in food supplies, for Vienna will be eaten out of house and home by the soldiers when they come back. I too suffer from chronic hunger."

It is now a week since we had the ¼-pint of milk due to us on our **ration cards**. I resolve to "hamster" (hoard food). During my husband's lifetime, I dared not do this. When he was seriously ill, I did it without his knowledge.

Sette Communi a division of territories in northeast Italy

Wilson, with his Fourteen Points On January 8, 1918, President Woodrow Wilson gave a speech calling for postwar peace in Europe. He summarized his message in Fourteen Points.

ration cards cards issued by the government during wartime that allowed individuals to receive a certain amount of food and other goods

I did not feel that I was becoming **demoralised**—on the contrary, I might almost say: Have I not the right to guard and protect the life of my family? For all its rigorous organisation, the State could not feed its citizens, and it cannot do so to-day. For a long time we have only been getting a part of the food due to us. The doctors have discovered that, even if we got the whole of our ration, this would only be sufficient to meet one-fourth of the food requirements of an adult person weighing **11 stone**.

. . . Now, at the end of the fourth year of war, when the Central Powers and their whole civilian population are like a besieged fortress cut off from all external supplies and without any hope of breaking through the hunger blockade, I am no longer disposed to sacrifice any more members of my family to the **Moloch** of war.

November 1, 1918
Wretched meals. Erni comes back.

Liesbeth, Wolfi, and I were seated at our wartime breakfast table. From a "hamstered" tin of milk I was spooning out the scanty rations for Liesbeth and Wolfi into bowls filled with hot water. After the spoon had been used, it was carefully scraped, so that not a drop of milk should be lost. Wolfi was then allowed to lick the spoon, which he did with great thoroughness and obvious enjoyment.

11 stone a unit of measurement used to calculate weight; 11 stone is equal to 154 pounds

Moloch a god to whom children were sacrificed

Fortunately the milk was sweetened. For months we have been getting only saccharine on our ration-cards, or very small portions of sticky, yellow, **unpalatable** raw sugar. The rations, if one gets them at all, are so small that it is impossible to meet one's sugar requirements, allowing one cup of tea a day. Tea and coffee I have in fact long since banished as luxurious stimulants without any nutritive value.

Extra Edition!

The old house-porter was standing outside our front door. It almost looked as though he were waiting for me. "Frau, a great surprise! The young gentleman has come home." "Which?" I seized his arm with a sense of mingled joy and alarm. "Why, Herr Erni!" I rushed up the stairs as fast as my feet would carry me, until I was completely out of breath. . . .

Erni, with a black bandage over both eyes, was seated at the piano. He looked very pale. His face was turned upwards, and an ecstatic smile played over his soft lips. He passed from the Mozart to a melody that was strange to me, but its wonderful, melancholy harmonies seemed to enrapture him.

I smoothed one of the wavy locks of hair that had been disarranged by the eye-bandage. He stopped playing and clutched his head with a low sigh. "It still hurts!" He stood up and felt for my hands. . . . And he told me how he and his men were repelling an aeroplane attack when a bomb dropped from an aeroplane exploded near them and killed seven of his men, while he was wounded in the left eye by a small splinter.

saccharine an artificial substitute for sugar that is used to sweeten foods

Frau term for a married German woman, usually used as "Mrs." is used in the English language

Herr a title of respect used for gentlemen in Germany, as "Mr." is used in the English language

As they were in an advanced and very inaccessible mountain position, he could not get to the ambulance until the next day. They sent him with the next batch of wounded to **Innsbruck**, where the Professor operated on him at once, but said that it would be a long time before he could use his eyes again, for the wounded eye had infected the sound one.

November 5, 1918
Erni's eyes.

Yesterday I took Erni to Professor X. at the Eye Clinic. While Erni was having a new bandage put on his eyes the Professor told me that he had practically no hope of saving his sight. The optic nerve was injured. Possibly an operation might be tried later, and so on. "But don't say anything about this to the patient; it is important to accustom one's self gradually to such a great misfortune." I could not speak a word, but I was filled with utter despair. "Dear Frau Martha, don't lose heart. I know that you are an energetic, devoted and unselfish mother. . . . I repeat that later on it may be worth while to try an operation." "What shall I say to him?" "That the cure will take some weeks, at the end of which time you are to come and see me again. Do not rob him of all hope." I was choked with rising tears. I stepped into the adjacent waiting room in order that my voice might not betray my distress to Erni.

Innsbruck a city in western Austria; capital city of the federal state of Tyrol

November 6, 1918

As we reached the streets leading to the railway stations, the scene completely changed. On the edge of the pavement soldiers returned from the Front were seated in long rows with their rucksacks: Many of them looked neglected and ailing. These crowds were more dense round the railway stations, where the square looked like some disorderly military camp. Although the weather was cold and stormy, many of the soldiers were only wearing their **threadbare** uniforms, without overcoats. Among the soldiers there were groups of civilians, and upon looking and listening more attentively, one suddenly discovered that a market had sprung up, though certainly without the **sanction** of the authorities. In this market, clothes, shoes, weapons, blankets and other still usable articles in the possession of the soldiers were being bartered for food. Money was refused, for what could anyone buy with money, when everything that is of practical value to us at present, such as foodstuffs and clothes, is subject to Government control and only obtainable in exchange for ration cards and frequently not even for these? The Government has done its best to provide some sort of shelter for the men returning from the Front, but many of them preferred to remain in the neighbourhood of the railway station because they hoped to secure an earlier opportunity of being sent back to their homes. Although most of the people, in spite of the brutalities they had experienced during the War, looked tired and peaceable, political agitators, who had remained in the Hinterland during the War, were already at work.

Hinterland a region that lies beyond an urban area

November 8, 1918
Failure of the meat supply.

The police were examining the ration cards of all the people in the queue to see whether they were entitled to horse-flesh. I estimated the crowd waiting here for a **meagre** midday meal at two thousand at least. Hundreds of women had spent the night here in order to be among the first and make sure of getting their bit of meat. . . .

They alarmed those standing at the back by telling them that there was only a very small supply of meat and that not half the people waiting would get a share of it. The crowd became very uneasy and impatient and, before the police on guard could prevent it, those standing in front organised an attack on the hall which the salesmen inside were powerless to repel. Everyone seized whatever he could lay his hands on, and in a few moments all the eatables had vanished, as though devoured by a hungry swarm of locusts. . . .

Although the German armies are still fighting on the western Front, the War is ended for us Austrians and has given place to an armistice. After four years that seemed as if they would never end, I have to mourn a terrible war sacrifice: my husband and Otto dead, Erni deprived of his sight; Rudi a cripple with only half a leg; Karl utterly changed owing to his head wound and perhaps not sane; Liesbeth weak and ailing for lack of nourishing food, Aunt Bertha bedridden with bone-softening due to under-nourishment.

December 3, 1918

The position of the housewives is becoming more and more difficult. Four weeks have elapsed since the Armistice, but there is not the slightest improvement, or hope of improvement, in the food situation. . . .

Hungry and underfed as we are, a well-heated room has become more than ever a necessity. Ill-nourished and always half-frozen, we have not the strength to resist infectious diseases, such as influenza, tuberculosis, etc. . . .

We are now only allowed to burn one 25-candle-power electric bulb in the whole flat. We get one candle and ¼ litre petroleum per week. The use of the gas-heater has been cut down to one hour daily. If the legal allowance of gas is exceeded, the supply is ruthlessly cut off. The heating of bath-water is an impossibility, and soap is becoming difficult to procure. I have to heat up small quantities of water on the little iron stove. We have said good-bye to baths. The shops have been ordered to close at four o'clock in the afternoon.

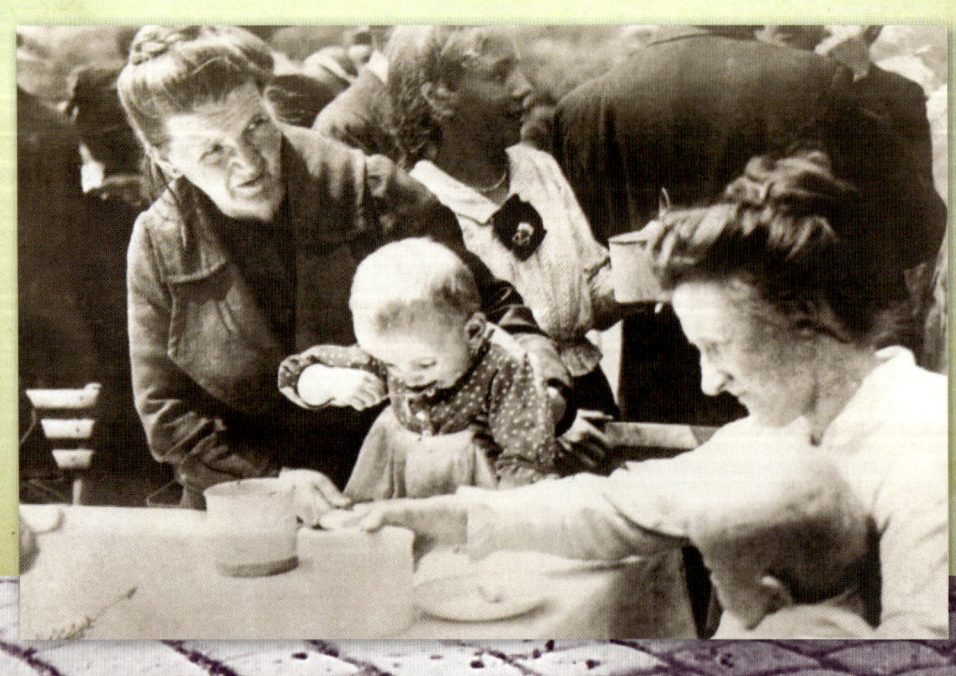

December 21, 1923

The **Peace of St. Germain** has been signed. In the abnormal economic position in which we were placed it was received with apathy. . . . This peace has not brought any alleviation to the Viennese housewives. . . .

January 2, 1924

We, too, belong today to the new poor. There is light, heat, food, and drink in Vienna to-day. Everything can be bought for the new **schillings**. If one has them! But who is lucky enough to have them? The middle class has been reduced to a **proletariat**. I, too, can escape from starvation only if I find new sources of income. So I must once more struggle and worry. Once more I must thrust all spiritual and cultural interests into the background, and like all the rest who find themselves in my position hunt for schillings in order to keep body and soul together.

Peace of St. Germain signed on September 10, 1919, by the Allies (France, Great Britain, and Russia) and Austria-Hungary; it declared the Austro-Hungarian Empire be dissolved, as well as various war reparations

schillings a form of currency in Austria

proletariat lowest social and economic class of a community; the laboring class

Harry Frieman

HARRY Frieman was born in Russia on December 5, 1888, and subsequently moved to Baltimore, Maryland. He was working as an expert tailor and insurance clerk when he was drafted in 1917, a month before his twenty-ninth birthday.

Frieman's experiences cover the last year of the war. After being drafted and sent for training at Camp Meade in Maryland, he set sail for France as part of the 313th Machine Gun Company. He and his company were sent to the front lines of the war as part of the Meuse-Argonne Offensive, also called the Battle of Argonne Forest. The battle was the largest in U.S. military history, involving 1.2 million American soldiers along the entire Western front, and lasted for forty-seven days. It was the last battle of the war.

Frieman kept a daily diary the entire time he was in the service. His entries show the hardships that soldiers faced while on the front, including miserable weather; lack of food, water, and shelter; and constant artillery fire. After the war, he finished his military service in France and was sent back to the states. His heir, Jack Frieman, donated his war memorabilia and diary to the U.S. Veterans History Project.

Nov. 16, 1917 Drafted and sent to Camp Meade, Md.

Sat. July 6, 1918 Left Camp Meade at 5:30 p.m. on P. R. B. via Baltimore Philadelphia to Jersey City.

Tue., July 9 Convoy left at 7 a.m. Sea very calm. Sighted whale and porpoises. Storm coming. Raining. Sunset beautiful.

Wed., July 10 Salt water shower. Ship drill 7 p.m. Ship sighted 7:30 p.m. Guns aiming at it.

Mon, July 15 Saw land at 10:40 a.m. At Brest 12:45 p.m. Scenery in harbor beautiful. Placed on small boat about 5 p.m. and landed at 6 p.m. Marched about three hours to rest camp. We had two meals a day on boat and very good.

Thur, July 18 Standing around fire to keep warm to 4 a.m. Marched to R. R. Station. Aboard freight car 7:30 a.m.

Sat, July 20 Still on train. Pass through tunnel, 3 miles long. Saw many German prisoners.

Mon, Aug. 26 Drill hours changed. Drill 7:30 to 2:30.

Fri, Aug. 30 Drill as usual. Received auto guns.

Tues, Sept. 3 Drill as usual. Out throwing hand grenades.

Fri, Sept. 6 Drill as usual. Medical inspection. Evening beginning of **Rosh Hashanah**. Services held in Y.M.C.A.

Sat, Sept. 7 Evening we received orders to draw emergency rations and move Sunday.

Thurs, Sept. 12 We turned in all personal belongings and prepared to move. We pulled out at 5 p.m. Hiked one hour with pack and 500 rounds of **ammunition**. Laid on wet ground to 12 p.m. waiting for trucks.

Rosh Hashanah a Jewish high holiday that marks the beginning of the Jewish New Year

Fri, Sept. 20 **Huns** done little shelling on our lines. None hurt—a few air battles during the day. We received order to move that night. We hiked for two hours to some woods and slept in field (cold). We were somewhere in the Argonne Forest.

Thurs, Sept. 26 At midnight our artillery on whole front. Twenty-six hundred cannons of all sizes opened a **barrage** and continued to fire to 5:30 a.m. At that time we went over the top. The signal corps sent up a screen of smoke, which was like a wall in front of us so the Huns can't see us. We advanced a little and were caught in an **M. G. nest**. It was hard to advance on account of the ground all tore up. We had very few **casualties**.

Fri, Sept. 27 At day break we start again over No Man's Land. The weather very bad—cold, raining. We had to advance under artillery and M. G. We had to get into shellholes with water above our knees. This morning we cleaned out many M. G. nests—captured many prisoners and took Montfaucon (1,200 ft. above sea level). It was one of the best observation posts the Huns had. This is where the Crown Prince viewed the Battle of Verdun in 1916 when 100,000 soldiers gave their lives. The town was in ruins—not a building left. That afternoon the Huns were to start a counter attack. We took up a defensive position in case of attack, but they failed and we advanced further under heavy fire and gas shells of all kinds.

Hun a derogatory name for a German

M. G. nest short for machine gun nest, a round pit manned by machine gunners

Sun, Sept. 29 At daybreak we started off again. We went very fast and our Artillery couldn't keep up with us. We crossed many hills and we were under observation of the Huns. We had many casualties in the 313th Reg. John Ryan, the best liked man of our company, was killed.

Mon, Sept. 30 The whole regiment stood in line for about two hours in mud over the shoe tops waiting for a cup of hot coffee as we had nothing to eat for a few days. When it reached our company there was no more left, so we had nothing that night.

During this drive, we had emergency rations of four boxes **hard tack**, one pound **corn willie**. We ate that and had one hot meal Sunday midnight. That is all we ate on account of our kitchen could not keep up with us. We had a canteen of water when we started and we did not get to any water until Sunday afternoon. We were lucky that the Huns in their retreat failed to cut off the water. Until Sunday most of the men were drinking water out of shell holes, taking a chance, as most of the holes were full of gas. We had many gas attacks. We wore our masks at times when the gas was heavy. At times we would go right on without them. The weather was cold and raining nearly every day. We had hardly any sleep as we had to lay in water and mud—cold out and no cover of any kind.

hard tack hard, unsalted biscuits
corn willie canned corned beef

Sat, Oct. 5 We took a good wash this morning as we haven't washed for many days and have not had our clothes off since Sept. 12th. Today is the first time that **cooties** have been found on some of the men in our company.

Mon, Oct. 7 We moved from here 5 p.m. Hiked to 10 p.m. The road was very bad—water and mud over the shoe tops. We stopped in dugouts with electric lights. Men take up their gun positions. Things quiet.

Tues, Oct. 8 Just a little **Boche** artillery fire and M. G. fire.

Thurs, Oct. 10 Artillery fire.

Fri, Oct. 11 Artillery and M. G. fire.

Sat, Oct. 12 Artillery and M. G. fire.

Sun, Oct. 13 Artillery battle. Huns threw many gas shells— casualties about seventy-five.

Tues, Oct. 22 At 4:30 a.m. the Huns sent over a large raiding party and opened an artillery and M. G. barrage, but they were run back.

Thurs, Oct. 24 About 2 a.m. the Huns sent over a heavy barrage of gas shells. They fell far to the left of us. No casualties. Quiet during day.

Thurs, Oct. 31 This evening at 6 p.m. we moved to another front where many hard battles have been fought. We passed through Death Valley under little shell fire, not knowing what a bad place this is. No casualties. We relieved the 26th Division.

cooties lice

Boche German

Fri, Nov. 1 This morning about 4 a.m. the Huns opened an artillery barrage. One man of our company was wounded. Our trenches were only about seventy-five yards away from the Boche trench. At some places it was closer; we had to whisper to each other so they did not hear us.

Sun, Nov. 3 This evening a **Dictaphone** was found in one of the dugouts. The Huns must have heard everything that was said in some dugouts. They found bombs under the floors.

Mon, Nov. 4 The usual barrage. This afternoon I started out to look for water as we had no water for three days. One of the boys and I started through an open field all torn up by shells and there were very many dead which we had to cross over. We found some water. On our way back, the Boche fired at us with M. G.s. We said, "Never again will we go there."

Dictaphone an audio-recording machine

Tues, Nov. 5 Usual barrage—morning, day, and evening. One shell blew up some of our ammunition and boxes, which were sitting outside of dugout.

Thurs, Nov. 7 Barrage same as always. While going to **Officers P.C.**, I noticed a box laying on ground and wires near by, and when we touched or stepped on wire, M. G. would open fire.

Fri, Nov. 8 We started out of woods 5 a.m. under barrage. We made double time, but two were wounded. We went back to hill where our kitchen is and rested for day. (This Ormont Woods is part of the "Belleau Woods" known as Hill 360 and Valley below as "Death Valley.") The Huns were about seventy-five yards from our gun positions. Their artillery had the exact range on every path in woods and valley and they would always open a barrage; at night their M. G. would always fire and they would keep on throwing up flairs. We would drop in the mud so they could not see us. Their artillery tore the woods up so bad that we couldn't find our way at night. Every time a flair would go up we would pick out a path and go a little further.

Every man in this woods was a nervous wreck. Water was very hard to get. Many days we had no water. Mess we had once a day on account of the danger to bring it up.

Sat, Nov. 9 This morning at 7 a.m. we started for another front. We hiked about four hours. We stopped on some road and couldn't go further on account of shell fire and being under Huns observation. We laid on road until 6 p.m. and hiked back to the place we started from and stopped over night.

Officers P.C. command post

Sun, Nov. 10 We marched to Hill on left side of Hill 360. The trenches at this place were very crowded with dead Germans, the most we have ever seen.

For the past few days the Huns have been retreating so fast that our boys could hardly keep up. They were nearly out of reach of our artillery all the time in these few days.

Mon, Nov. 11 This morning our artillery was to open a barrage from 9:30 to 10:30 a.m. and then we were supposed to go over the top. About 9 a.m. we were caught in Huns shell fire. Took our guns and ammunition off the carts and started to walk. It was very foggy, and we couldn't see over ten yards in front of us. We were caught in a barrage and had to hide behind a slope. The shells were bursting all around us. We were lucky that the ground was very soft and the shells stuck there and only threw a lot of mud over us. At 10:30 a.m. we received orders to open a M. G. barrage, but just as we set our guns up to fire, an officer passed by and said, "Boys, take your time. I have a message to stop firing 11 a.m." We could hardly believe it until we were told to stop firing at 11 a.m. and not to fire unless they fire. The last shots by both sides were fired exactly 11 a.m. The fog lifted about 12 noon and how lucky we were. We were caught in a trap with Huns on three sides of us, and Company A was only a few yards away from them. If the war would have kept up a few hours longer, there would not be many of us left to tell about it. That afternoon, we moved back of the Hill and took defensive positions. About 4 p.m. the Huns started to celebrate firing all kinds of sky rockets. They kept this up all night.

Conclusion

After the armistice in November 1918, it took seven months of negotiations at the Paris Peace Conference for the countries involved to create the first treaty. It was the Treaty of Versailles, signed on June 28, 1919—five years to the day after Archduke Franz Ferdinand was assassinated.

The Treaty of Versailles was the treaty between the Allies and Germany. It mandated that Germany take full responsibility for starting the war in 1914, and thus pay all damages and reparations to the winning countries—a vast sum meant to keep Germany weak. Germany had to surrender the colonies and most of its army, including both troops and machinery, such as airplanes. The Allies were allowed to keep its forces in Germany until the money had been paid back. The harsh terms of the treaty left Germany in a terrible economic depression and susceptible to the nationalistic calls of Adolf Hitler fourteen years later.

However, the Treaty of Versailles also created the League of Nations, which is similar to the United Nations that we have today. The principal goal of the League of Nations was to prevent future wars. It was a singular governing body through which countries could negotiate and settle arguments. After "the war to end all wars," the League of Nations tried to bring peace. Unfortunately, because it didn't have a military and relied solely on funding and sanctions from countries in the League, it was unable to prevent the next world war.

GLOSSARY

ammunition (am-yuh-NIH-shun) *noun* objects fired from guns or explosive devices used in war (page 23)

annexing (uh-NEK-sing) *verb* attaching or incorporating territory to a city, state, or country (page 2)

armistice (AR-mih-stis) *noun* an agreement between enemies to stop fighting (page 3)

artillery (ar-TIH-ler-ee) *noun* large firearms such as cannons, rockets, or guns (page 5)

barrage (buh-RAHZH) *noun* a furious and rapid projection of many things at once (page 24)

besieged (bih-SEEJD) *verb* overwhelmed with requests or crowds (page 13)

casualties (KA-zhul-teez) *noun* people who are hurt or killed during a war (page 24)

demoralised (dih-MOR-uh-lized) *verb* without hope (page 15)

despondent (dih-SPAHN-dent) *adjective* extremely discouraged or depressed (page 11)

dismal (DIZ-mul) *adjective* gloomy; not warm or cheerful (page 10)

incessantly (in-SEH-sent-lee) *adverb* without pause or interruption (page 14)

latter (LA-ter) *adjective* the second choice (page 6)

meagre (MEE-ger) *adjective* insufficient; not enough (page 19)

motley (MAHT-lee) *adjective* made up of various dissimilar parts (page 14)

regiment (REH-jih-ment) *noun* a military unit containing large groups of soldiers (page 6)

sanction (SANK-shun) *noun* official permission or approval (page 18)

threadbare (THRED-bair) *adjective* very thin or in poor condition (page 18)

trenches (TREN-chez) *noun* long, narrow ditches in the ground constructed to protect soldiers (page 3)

unpalatable (un-PA-luh-tuh-bul) *adjective* unpleasant, unappetizing, or distasteful (page 16)

ANALYZE THE TEXT
Questions for Close Reading

Use facts and details from the text to support your answers to the following questions and prompts.

- How did rationing affect people's lives? Use evidence from the texts to support your answer.

- Find text evidence to support the idea that war is destructive, not only to human lives but also to land and property.

- Compare and contrast the daily life of the two soldiers. Provide textual evidence and details.

- Find evidence from the text that describes events that took place after the war, and specifically, how these events continued to affect people in negative ways.

- During wartime, many people searched for ways to find normalcy and continue living as they had before the war. Find evidence in the text where this occurs.

Comprehension: Make Inferences

Good readers use clues from the text to make inferences about things that are not directly stated. For each of the authors in the text, find a sentence from one of their diary entries that alludes to the author's feelings toward the war. Then explain an inference you can make from that statement.

Inference	Text Evidence